TWO FULL PLATES

Learning *to be a Caregiver*

Fran Rogers

And let the beauty of the LORD our God be upon us,
And establish the work of our hands for us;
Yes, establish the work of our hands.
Psalm 90:17

TWO FULL PLATES
Learning to be a Caregiver

Unless otherwise indicated Scripture quotations
are from The Holy Bible, King James Version

fatherandfamily.com
godsgracegodsglory.com

Cover design by Danielle Camorlinga
and Vector.Designs
Special font by Michelle Dixon

Dedicated to my husband, Jerry,
who for fifty-four years has patiently cared for me
and taught me to care for others and to care for him.
The Lord has blessed us together,
to love each other and others as He has loved us.

CONTENTS

Introduction to Series

Several years ago I began writing a series of books in order to share what God was revealing to me through His Word and in my own life. The title *Little Books About the Magnitude of God* was fostered by the reality that what I write is usually longer than an article, but shorter than a regular length book. Since 2011 shorter articles have been shared on my blog at godsgracegodsglory.com.

There is a great contrast between what we can write about God, and God, Himself. Anything written is little, or nothing, compared to the person of God, who He is and what He does. Everything that I write comes from a grateful heart for the greatness of our God, our Creator and Father. Every book is meant to minimize the work of man, and to promote and magnify the person and work of God. There is much we can write about man, the creature, but it is all very small compared to what we can write about God. There is enough written by man about man without adding another book to his credit, but not enough written about God to His glory.

Writing originally to share a legacy with future generations of our family, the file has grown in great proportions, beyond what I had imagined. In my seventy-six years God's grace has continued to multiply, and to give me more to write about. My family agrees that what God gives us is to be shared with others beyond our family ties. So, according to His will and timing, these books will be published.

And we are writing these things so that our joy may be complete. 1 John 1:4 ESV

As the apostle John wrote of his experience of seeing and knowing Jesus Christ, we, with the same witness as others who know Him by faith, understand the apostle Peter's words, "Though you have not seen him, you love him. Though you do not now see him, you believe in him and rejoice with joy that is inexpressible and filled with glory, obtaining the outcome of your faith, the salvation of your souls."

It is my prayer that all that comes from my hands will be from Him, of Him, through Him, about Him, and all to His glory and praise. In this my joy and life in Christ is complete.

Hopefully those who read any little book of this series will share the same love, joy, and faith that cannot be expressed at my hands, by anything that I will write, but through personally knowing the only One who can work these in each of us ~ to His glory and our joy!

Fran Rogers ~ January 2016

Update: Since beginning this project I have committed to give the majority of profits from sales of our books to charity and missions. Any who purchase a book will be a participant in this vision of Father and Family Books. Visit our website fatherandfamily.com for more details, and to leave your email if you would like to receive updates on what we are doing, and news of other publications.

Preface

In God's sovereignty and providence we see His plans for our creation. His plans are not always what we would have chosen for ourselves. Given the option we would most often disapprove of His choices. In our human nature we think our own thoughts and wish for ourselves the life that suits our inclinations. Even the regenerate man does not choose the role of the servant's life. If God advertised for servants, He would get very few applicants.

Creation is not our heavenly Father's only work, but as our Redeemer, He recreates us to reveal and fulfill His purpose in each of us. The Lord God gives us a new heart, and this heart has to be trained for the life He has planned for us. As a new creature in Christ, we are trained for the servant's role.

The desire to draft and perhaps publish a series of books about God's grace was developed through His working in my own life, and my writing for the last twenty-five years. Some advise writers not to write about their personal lives, but God's working in my life is the reason for my writing. The purpose of this first book in the series *Little Books About the Magnitude of God* is to show how I have experienced the work of Christ in my life as a caregiver, with the desire to help other caregivers. Other little books in the series spring from this one.

As a younger adult I might have been diagnosed as bi-polar. Even now, I would probably be seen as one with obsessive-compulsive behavior. Christ in me and my circumstances has humbled me, and enabled me to get past myself so as to minister to others. It is His Holy Spirit that continues to grow me in grace and *the knowledge of our Lord Jesus Christ,* to humble me (whatever it takes), and to praise Him in the process.

The expression, "I have a full plate," is used often when people are asked to help someone, and they do not have time to spare from their full schedules. That is the idea for the title of this book, considering that with my own children, grandchildren, my mother with dementia, and my husband who is an amputee, I have not only prepared two plates for food at meals, but also come to care for them as part of my life and purpose.

What I share first is that I know Christ as my caregiver, from whom I am still learning ~ "Even as the Son of man came not to be ministered unto, but to minister."

Chapter 1

CHILDREN ARE TAUGHT TO SERVE

And, ye fathers, provoke not your children to wrath:
but bring them up in the nurture
and admonition of the Lord.
Ephesians 6:4

Never really enjoying my job as a dishwasher it was still my first duty when I came home from elementary school every weekday. Both my parents worked, so when I got home every afternoon I had to wash the breakfast dishes before making the beds or doing anything else. Although soaking dishes all day makes them easier to wash, I have learned that they don't have to soak all day. It helps to empty the sink of dirty dishes during the day, so that they don't pile up before dinnertime. It must have been this early training that enables me now to enjoy this duty. Even when I am tired it seems to come naturally. A new day is much easier to face when I walk into a clean kitchen. The simple tasks of dishwashing and bed-making have always been a part of my life.

We neglect the training our children need when we, as parents, do all the work, or hire it to be done. They, like many of us, misunderstand the purpose of the chores that need to be done and the role that each of us has in doing them.

We never know what awaits us later in life, and what we are being trained for. Although we learn in the process, dealing with adversity in adulthood is somewhat easier when we have been taught to serve the family and others.

Paul taught the early Christians that Christ is the head of the husband; and the husband is head of his wife. (1 Corinthians 11:3) Together they teach their children, by example, to become husbands and wives (Lord willing). Whether or not they marry, they will, as God's children, be servants to His family. *The nurture and admonition of the Lord* includes bringing them up to minister as He ministered.

As the husband serves His family, so he serves the Lord, being an example to his family, as they are taught to minister to others. As the wife is a helpmate to her husband, she is an example to the daughters. Together they fulfill God's purpose for their creation and redemption through the family.

From this institution, families minister to each other in the church, and to others to whom He directs us. Individual ministry, the ministry of the family, and ministry within the church are God's means of light and revelation to the world of His kingdom. When we pray for *His name to be hallowed, His kingdom to come, and His will to be done here on earth,* we can expect that He will use us in answer to our requests. He puts hands and feet to our prayers.

Never would I have thought that spending lonely afternoons in a small kitchen washing dishes would help prepare me to fulfill God's purpose in my life and bring Him glory.

Chapter 2

PARENTS LEARN TO SERVE

For the children ought not to lay up for the parents,
but the parents for the children.
2 Corinthians 12:14

When Jerry and I married in 1961 he settled into an eight-to-five job as an industrial engineer with Burlington Industries in St. Pauls, North Carolina. His work with subsequent employers, Playtex, and Her Majesty, kept him at home the first twelve years. When he started working for Coats and Clark Thread Co. in the Industrial Division, he was out of town two or three days a week. We had moved to the Atlanta area from Greenville, S.C., three months after Jerry's mother died unexpectedly. As Andy, our son, began middle school, and Lee, our daughter, began second grade we were happy for the new job, and a new house. Neither of us knew from experience how families worked together when the father was absent from the home. Our parents had local jobs; our fathers were the head of the home; our mothers worked, and both shared the responsibilities for training their children.

Jerry's absence changed the schedule we were used to. We both had new jobs. He enjoyed the traveling, his new job, and the time he had with the family. My responsibilities doubled on the days that he was gone. It was not so difficult to begin with, but as Andy and Lee became challenged in school, and in new relationships, I faced the unprepared task of leadership and discipline, not just for them, but also for myself. Jerry and I did not always agree on discipline ~ theirs or mine. As most mothers who deal with this dual responsibility, I found that it was not easy for us, or the children to switch gears when the father leaves, and comes home. If he had known the effects of his being away, he might have found another job that would have kept him home. In the first twelve years Jerry had three jobs (without traveling) in four states. In his last job he traveled for almost thirty years; then retired.

Solving My Personal Problems

As I was reviewing this chapter I realized that my problems did not begin when Jerry started this new job. Years before, when I was plagued with headaches, my doctor prescribed Triavil, a mild anti-depressant, which he said would enable me to see "through rose-colored glasses." Though I did not understand what he meant, I took the medication. My headaches stopped, and I became confident in my life for the first time. But my confidence was in myself and what I was able to do. My accomplishments were not by faith in God. Joining the church and being baptized in my childhood had not prepared me for adulthood. There was no "Christ in me" to enable me to live victoriously through the difficult times.

Basically, during those times, Jerry had three children to deal with. Those were what I now call my "domineering" years. In order to get my point across, (which I thought was best for the children) Jerry and I went through some stormy times. It was difficult even for me to know what was right for myself. I withdrew and was sometimes in my own little world.

I continued taking the anti-depressant for ten years. I became very industrious, sewing everything from draperies to clothes - even sport coats for Jerry and Andy. So much sewing ruined my shoulders, so I have not done much sewing since then. I was caught up in one thing, and then another, as I found I could do anything I set my mind to. When we moved with Jerry's new job, the children in school, and the new house in shape, I sat one day on our front steps, watching the house being built next door. Having grown up and watching my dad build houses, I said, "I could do that." And so I did. We had a few thousand dollars from the sale of Jerry's parents' house after his mother died, and we bought two lots across the street. I sub-contracted to the contractors that our builder used.

During this time I decided to wean myself from the anti-depressant. Successful with this, and using my knowledge from a decorating course, I started a decorating business, selling draperies, furniture, carpet, etc. When I ran into problems balancing the two jobs which I operated from home, I found that Transcendental Meditation would give me the ability to accomplish all that I wanted to do. I convinced the whole family that it would be good for us all. Lee and I were the only two that continued this practice, which worked for both of us. Even so, after a period of time, I began to wonder whether this was actually a good thing. Research led me to a book written by a Hindu who had become a Christian. He explained the origin and process of T.M. Understanding that I really did not want to be my own god, though this meditation worked for me, I stopped this practice.

Doing my own thing, though it was mostly while the children were in school, was my solution to the two full plates handed to me. It did not help me to be a better parent or give me wisdom in how to discipline, as I should. I did not understand the compulsive behavior of trying to do so many things at one time. On those two plates there was sometimes "crow" to eat. I was not the wife or mother that God had wanted me to be. But the Lord was in control, sovereign over all, and in His providence was continuing to train me to serve in difficult situations.

Heartwork

As Jerry traveled with his job, I looked for means to handle the roles that I wanted to fill. In the 80's the Lord began to draw me to His Word. As I continued to buy and renovate older homes I began a new interest in the things of God. We were members of a Baptist church where I sang in the choir and played for a children's choir. After a few years I was directing the children's choir. Then I started teaching ninth grade Sunday School. This seemed to be my calling at the time, and I gave up the building and decorating business to devote myself to the church. In time I was writing curriculum for the children's choir, middle school Sunday School, and youth discipleship groups. A few years later I began teaching a women's class what I had been learning from God's Word.

It was when I was studying and sharing the letters that John had written to the churches, in the Book of Revelation, that the Lord began doing a work in my heart. In the letter to the church at Ephesus he wrote, "I know thy works, and thy labour, and thy patience, and how thou canst not bear them which are evil: And hast borne, and hast patience, and for my name's sake hast laboured, and hast not fainted. Nevertheless I have somewhat against thee, because thou hast left thy first love. "

The Lord knew my works and the roles that I had taken on. The gift for teaching was from Him, but the work was my own. What John wrote to the early church brought conviction that I had not left this "first love," but that I had never known this "first love." From here He brought me to seek this "first love." Knowing it was Christ, the Son of God, who was giving John the things to write, I had to cease being a teacher of God's Word, to pray and wait for this "first love" ~ Christ, Himself.

As I relinquished all the responsibilities I had taken on, I prayed and studied God's Word. For the first time I knew what it meant to wait on God. Instead of making my life what I thought it ought to be, I sought Christ, by His Spirit, to work in me. If I was going to live in obedience to Him or to teach His Word, I knew I needed Him. I learned that it is one thing to know what you know from reading, which is only in the mind, but the truth of God's Word can only be effective as it comes from the heart. I learned that the best teachers are the ones who have experienced what they are teaching. The key verse of the middle-school curriculum I had done years before was Proverbs 3:5; *Trust in the Lord with all your heart, and lean not unto your own understanding.* Now He was bringing me to it, not as a writer or teacher, but as a sinner in need of mercy and truth, which comes only through His Son, Jesus Christ. From Proverbs 3: 3-4 we read, *Let not mercy and truth forsake thee: bind them about thy neck; write them upon the table of thine heart: So shalt thou find favour and good understanding in the sight of God and man.*

As Andrew Murray wrote in *Waiting on God*, the heart, not knowing what it is looking or waiting for, seeks; "the mind finds and brings to the heart what is needful." It is the heart where love finds its place. It is the *new heart* that the Lord gives, filled with His love for us that is impossible for us to leave. From this new heart given on a summer afternoon, on August 28, 1992, He has been writing love letters to me ever since. In His own timing, His Word, by the power of His Holy Spirit changed me, with a *new birth, to grow in grace and the knowledge of our Lord Jesus Christ ~ to grow up into Christ.* Since then I can say that He *bought* me (before I ever knew Him), *sought* me, (as my Shepherd), *caught* me (not only by His rod and staff, but by His love), *brough*t me (led me by the still waters, and restoring my soul, to the paths of righteousness), and has *taugh*t me (continually speaking His word of truth.)

By this time Andy and Lee were in high school. They were doing what they had been taught, seeking their purpose and work in the world, learning to be independent. I had given them all that I had been given. I had always said I did not want to work outside the home and was there when they were home, and as best as I knew, I gave them my full attention. Sometimes my plates were full from my own business outside the home, which included my church life. Giving up choir practice on Wednesday nights was my first attempt to fulfill my role as a mother and a caregiver while Jerry was away from home. Rarely do we see the role of a parent as a caregiver, but we are caregivers to any who are not out on their own, able to support themselves. Children fit this category as long as they are under our roof. This realization did not come until years later.

Temptations are still a part of my life, and I expect they always will be here on this earth. God's people still live in a wilderness, though He has brought us out of "the pit" (See *The Pit and the Wilderness*). Our greatest temptations are those of self, the flesh, and the things of this world. The greatest defense against these is humility, the humility of Christ that is instilled in us by His Spirit. I was not a humble wife or mother when my children were home. But, this is my continual desire, and He is present to humble me at every turn. It is not a natural trait, but a supernatural phenomenon that He has to work in us. He has been doing His work all these years in my role as a caregiver.

Chapter 3

GRANDCHILDREN ARE GOOD TEACHERS

A good man leaves an inheritance
to his children's children:
Proverbs 13:22

My new heart, new birth, new spirit, and new life that began in August, 1992, were given only a few weeks before our first grandchild was born. Ansley was a new ray of sunshine for us as middle-agers. My intent after giving up teaching was that I would never be responsible for any more children. I had brought up my own, taught others, now had my own life, and did not want this responsibility again. God's timing again was perfect. With the new heart came a new perspective of children, their purpose, and how parents and grandparents relate to them and the role that God has planned for them. I had not known that Lee would return to work after she had children. Her training as a physical therapist was so as to have a flexible career that she could return to whenever her children were out of school.

Because she felt the need to supplement their income, she decided to work part-time three days a week. When Brad's mother agreed to keep Ansley two days a week, Lee was in need of someone to keep her one other day.

I agreed to the one day, but afterward Brad's parents moved to Alabama, so Lee needed someone to keep her those two days. Jerry wanted me to keep Ansley all three days, because he thought that if Lee needed to work that I should be the one to help her. Having been Ansley's caregiver for one day a week, it seemed only right that I should be her caregiver for all three days. So, from the time she was three months old, I devoted my time to her. After a while, Lee decided to work only two days, so I then had an extra day for my own time.

New Convictions

After Andy and Lee married, I spent more time in prayer, especially in intercession, in Bible study, and writing more of what I was learning of this new life in Christ. We sold our home and downsized to a new home. Moving away and leaving our former church I met with two other friends for weekly prayer for seven years. When one of them moved we disbanded.

When Ansley was 3 ½, Kourtney was born. Ansley still depended on me to serve her plate, and Kourtney's bottle was Lee's pumped breast milk. With Jerry's absence in traveling with his job, the girls soon became my life. This conviction came during my prayer and study time one morning as I was reading the fourteenth chapter of Luke.

*If any man come to me, and hate not his father, and mother, and wife, and **children**, and brethren, and sisters, yea, and his own life also, he cannot be my disciple.* Luke 14:26

I was devastated; and so was Lee when I told her that evening that I could not keep them anymore. Jerry was very upset when he learned that he would not be able to see them on the days he was home. Brad's sister kept them that summer. In the fall I took on the responsibility again, but with a new understanding.

I realized that as long as they were in my care I should be teaching them. Besides teaching Kourtney during the school year, after Ansley started school, we began a series of study during the summer months called *Summer of Psalms*. Ansley was six and Kourtney was three years old when we started our first summer with Psalm 100. We used seven of the Psalms 100, 23, 121, 8, 146, and 149 (repeating the seven) for fourteen summers, putting these seven into workbooks. We memorized each Psalm, repeating them each year, building on the study of these Psalms as each related to the gospel. Ansley did the study for ten years; Kourtney did the study for all fourteen years. Olivia did the study for eight years; Emma, for seven years.

Kourtney was in kindergarten when Olivia was born. The following summer Ansley, Kourtney, and Olivia stayed with me the two days Lee worked. Olivia was two when Emma was born, so I kept both of them all year. During these times I had five full plates. When they were ten we allowed them to fill their own plates (food) with the understanding that they did not take more than they would eat.

The things of God that I did not have to teach my own children were given years later so that they could be part of a legacy to future generations.

How blessed we have been to share the treasures of His kingdom with our grandchildren.

Chapter 4

PARENTS AND CHILDREN LEARN TOGETHER

*Precious in the sight of the Lord
is the death of his saints.*
Psalm 116:15

Ansley was almost two years old when we learned that my dad had esophageal cancer. He was given a month to live, but died three weeks later. I wrote about that experience in *One Month to Live ~ A Father's Last Words*. Those last three weeks with Daddy and Mother are unforgettable as the Lord was directing the whole scenario. It was sad and wonderful, amazing and unfathomable, all at the same time.

I had no life of my own, none for Jerry, my children or grandchild. As I write this, I don't even remember who kept Ansley those three weeks. The only place I remember is being by my father's side. At the same time, I was there to encourage my mother, who was losing the husband to whom she had been married for over 60 years. My presence allowed her to deal with the situation without having to make major decisions on her own. She never really understood what was going on. She was at first in denial that Daddy had cancer, but she did what she needed to do.

Mother's Example

I was doing what I had to do as I had learned from my mother. She had been an example for me as she had cared for Daddy for many years. Because he had been ill for so long, and Mother was beginning to "wear down" in the process, we knew that "something had to give." She was 80 years old, still caring for Daddy, three weeks before he died at the age of 85. She had been his helpmate since she was fifteen years old.

She had sacrificed also for my brother and his children, keeping them while my sister-in-law worked a fulltime job. Only in my latter years have I been able to thank God for both my parents and for all that they did for me. I had wished that things had been different in my childhood, but the Lord continues to show me that He is sovereign, and has always been working all things to His glory and our good.

Mother said after she and Daddy retired that if she could do it over she would not have worked, but would have stayed home.

Watching God Work

My dad could not eat during those three weeks, and he had chosen not to be fed intravenously. He learned to humble himself, giving in to whatever was left for him. We all learned to accept what the Lord had planned, and to depend on Him for everything, every day. We as a family learned to give up our own desires; our own lives, for my dad. Since I was there, everyone else worked his or her job during the day. My brother and nephew took turns at night staying with Dad and the sitter.

His death was different from any I have ever known. I walked part way *through the valley of death* with him, knowing that the Lord had been present and active as He was bringing Daddy home to be with Him. I saw a sick man relinquish his fight against death to be at peace with the thoughts of his final *rest in the Lord*. He stopped trying, and began to watch the proceedings around him. The Lord blessed his request and our prayers for mercy. Daddy never needed morphine or any other pain medication. He simply passed from this life into glory with the Father on Monday, Labor Day, September 5, 1994.

Chapter 5

LEARNING TO SERVE UNDER DURESS

If any man or woman that believes have widows,
let them relieve them,
and let not the church be charged;
that it may relieve them that are widows indeed.
1 Timothy 5:16

The three weeks that I spent at Daddy's bedside taught me much that I would carry over into the remainder of my life. Learning not to take life and family for granted, I saw each day with different meaning. I sought to know how to serve the Lord and others more than I had ever before. I did not know, however, how much Mother still needed us after Daddy died. A few years afterward she seemed to be doing well, except that she heard an occasional voice outside the window, which she said was Daddy calling her.

She did not seem scared, living by herself, although she had never lived alone until then. Had we known what we learned later, we would have brought her to live with us before she became independent. Whenever we called to check on her, she seemed to be well, and said she didn't need anything. After eight years she gradually became confused, scared, and paranoid. Dementia set in before we had much warning ~ there were a few signs that we did not think significant, such as forgetfulness, loss of hearing, misplacing or hiding important documents, etc. Instead of being the family that she needed and trusted, we became the enemy. It was not until she was admitted to the hospital with Bronchitis two consecutive New Year's Eves that we realized we had to make plans for her care ~ namely, to be her caregiver.

Jerry had retired two years earlier; and between adjusting to his being home, and still caring for grandchildren, we did not know if having Mother here would work for any of us. Under duress, I spent time in counseling with our pastor. Biblically, I knew this is what I should do, but I needed more than what the Bible says about families caring for each other. Taking care of Daddy was a three-week calling. Taking care of grandchildren for two days a week was a joy ~ they were trainable, disciplined, knew how to obey, and went home at night. I didn't know if I could handle another plate.

"Lord, you know that I don't know how to care for a patient with dementia. How do I do this?"

His answer did not come then, but as each day presented the challenges, we prayed more fervently and more often. In obedience we brought her home with us from the hospital. From there it was mostly downhill for 4 ½ years for her. We endured with her, but not always gracefully. Not wanting to dishonor her I purposefully am not sharing in detail those bad times. But the Lord was gracious to us all.

Mother's best times were with the grandchildren. Olivia, Emma, and Andy's children, Nathan and Leila, were attentive to her childlike spirit, and would take her by the hand and lead her upstairs to the playroom to be with them. They were caregivers, even as Jerry and I were.

We would prepare Mother's plate at mealtime. She often said, "That's too much." Though it was not completely full, we would tell her, "Eat what you can." Usually, she ate all that we gave her.

In quiet times, other than prayer time, which were not often, I tried to remember Mother as she used to be. All I could muster was the thought of her life in giving to others. Besides her service to her family and her church, she was the neighbor that went door to door, or called everyone, whenever someone needed something, to plan meals, to find donations for those in need. Gradually, the memories of Mother's last years are fading. It is good to think of her again as she used to be.

Mother, like my dad, was a recipient of the Lord's mercy. Even in her forgetfulness of who Jesus was, or a knowledge of God that she could communicate to anyone else, she would walk through the house at night saying, "God, be merciful to me." As her body was declining she was admitted to a nursing home four weeks before she died. Her mind and spirit were in turmoil until her last three days, when she lay unresponsive. Knowing that the time was close, I prayed that she would not die on Monday, my birthday. That night Jerry and I sat with her while the Lord blessed to retain His Spirit with her until 12:38, when she died peacefully, immediately after I recited Psalm 23.

In response to the news of Mother's death, the comment was made that my life had been put on hold during my care for her, "Now you can go on with your life." My gentle response was "Caring for her was my life, the role God had given me."

My life has never been put on hold; it is always going forward. The Lord is more real, more powerful, and leading me every step in the circumstances of my life to "deny self, to take up my cross daily, and to follow Him." In all of this is the true joy of the Christian life, experiencing the suffering and the sacrifice for Him, and tasting of His glory while still here on earth.

My life was not my own the three weeks before my dad died. It was not my own the 4 ½ years that Jerry and I cared for my mother. It has never been my own; it has taken the years of my life as a caregiver to understand this.

The Interim

At church, three days after Mother's funeral, we learned that our pastor and four other families were leaving to plant a new church in Tennessee. This was another thing that was difficult to deal with, but this too was part of God's plan to teach me and to humble me.

Chapter 6

SERVING FOR LIFE

And the Lord God said,
It is not good that the man should be alone;
I will make him an help meet for him.
Genesis 2:18

At the time of Mother's death my health was at a low ebb. It was by God's strength that I was able to endure her last year. Within the next five weeks, Jerry and I took care of the things that must be attended to after a loved one is gone. How gracious the Lord was during that time to renew my strength (knowing the next trial that would come). Most of our time was spent in Thomaston, clearing everything with Social Security. Because she and

Daddy had signed the deed to their home to my brother and me many years before he became ill, Mother had no property to dispose of, and my brother bought our interest in the house, where he and his wife lived until he died in 2011.

There was hardly any time for grieving for her before the Wednesday afternoon a month later, when Jerry experienced excruciating pain in the calf of his left leg.   He said that he had been experiencing pain before then.   He had ignored it because of having to help care for Mother.

Calling for an appointment with his cardiologist, he was scheduled for the next day, at which time he could only see the physician's assistant, who ordered a CT Scan. An appointment was scheduled for him to come back on Monday to see the cardiologist, and find out the results of the scan.   Until Monday I could not understand why Jerry went to the cardiologist instead of another doctor.

Jerry insisted that I was not needed to accompany him for his Monday appointment either. He called me at intervals to let me know the progress of the doctor's orders. He was scheduled for an angiogram at the hospital that afternoon. Because there were no beds available, he had to check in through the emergency room, waiting until five o'clock for his appointment there. Every call to me during the day was with his assurance that I did not need to be there, but finally he agreed for me to come, and to call Andy and Lee, and others who would pray for the outcome.

I drove to the hospital around four o'clock, found him, and waited with him for the angiogram. Afterward, the cardiologist took me into the room where they read the x-rays, and showed me the blockage of the main artery from Jerry's groin to his leg. The cardiologist then left Jerry in the hands of a vascular surgeon, who assured us that a simple procedure would remove the blood clot and allow the blood flow to his leg.

Leaving the recovery room to call Andy and Lee took only a few minutes. Returning to be with Jerry, the surgeon informed us that they had just gotten the results of the CT Scan, which showed an aneurysm in the upper part of the leg. With this new information it was decided that this was the cause of the blood clot in the groin and the blockage of the artery. Jerry was then scheduled for surgery on Tuesday at five, with the plans to clean the artery at the groin area and by-pass the aneurysm to allow the blood flow.

Emergency Surgery

Tuesday, Jerry was in surgery from 8:00 to 11:00 P.M. We knew something was not right when the surgery took so long. It was supposed to take only an hour to an hour and a half. Finally the surgeon met us in the waiting room with the news that Jerry had severe arteriolosclerosis. Because his pain had not been to the level that was expected for such an advanced stage, he was amazed at the blood clotting in Jerry's leg and believing it to be in others parts of his body as well. He did three incisions: one in the groin, one just below the knee, and one at the ankle. The two lower ones he opened to try to clean as far as he could in both directions of the artery. He said that if this was not successful (and he did not seem hopeful) the only alternative was amputation. The next 24 hours would prove yes, or no.

We were not at all prepared for this. Andy and Lee comforted me as my tears flowed. I never thought about how they were affected by this news. Our pastor, a friend from our church, and a family from our church, were there with us.

Andy, Lee, and I got something to eat while they prepared to take Jerry to intensive care overnight. After seeing him, we left about 2:00 A.M. Lee came home with me for the night.

We met back at the hospital Wednesday morning to wait with Jerry. A CT Scan showed "no blood flow" in the main artery. The only blood to the leg at this point was through the small collateral arteries. Plans were made to send Jerry home in a couple of days to see what would happen as the incisions healed.

Before the surgery Jerry had to stop taking Coumadin (blood thinner), which he takes for his heart. After his surgery he was given Heparin, a liquid blood thinner, through an IV, and after two days, also started back on the Coumadin, hoping this would increase blood flow to his leg. This caused a dormant ulcer to hemorrhage for several days before they knew what was happening. He had an endoscopy, at which time they could not cauterize the ulcer.

After he was taken off the blood thinners, with the danger of less blood flow to the leg, he remained in the hospital for two weeks, receiving blood transfusions, and gaining back some of his strength. These were his hallucination days. He would have to explain this phenomenon to you.

My strength was again waning. Hours in the hospital, the 30-minute drive there and back every day, was wearing on me. Those days were some of the loneliest; coming home to an empty house at night was testing my faith. Lee offered for me to stay with them, but it was easier to come home, get a shower and fall into bed. What was happening seemed a nightmare. Rest did not come easy, but looking to and depending on the Lord became easier. He was my only hope.

I brought Jerry home on Monday, October 2. The surgeon said that it might be possible Jerry could live with things as they were. It would depend on how much blood the collateral arteries could provide, and how much pain Jerry could endure. He already called Jerry his "miracle man" because of his pain tolerance.

For three weeks a physical therapist came three times a week to help him learn to walk with crutches.

The incision at the groin healed in due time, but the other two did not. The one at the ankle was worse than the one at the knee. I had to start dressing the wounds because of the drainage. The pain was getting worse, and we were back in the surgeon's office every week.

On Friday, October 19, with Jerry's big toe turning blue, and beginning to drain, the surgeon said that we did not need to wait much longer before amputating. Before surgery we met with a prosthetist in the doctor's office to discover possibilities for the use of prosthesis after the surgery. They told us of the possibility of amputating below the knee, which would give Jerry more mobility with a prosthesis. We would be taking a chance, however, in case blood flow was not good. Jerry was asked what his projection would be; what he would want to do afterward. The only answer he could think of at the time was that he might be able to cut the grass, and do what he could to maintain the yard.

Amputation

On Tues. October 24, 2006, Jerry was anesthetized for the fourth time in five weeks---two for surgery, two for endoscopies for the ulcer. We did not know what to expect, but decided, with guidance, that a below-the-knee amputation was worth the risk, hoping and praying that he would not have to have another amputation later.

This surgery did not take nearly as long as the by-pass. He was given royal treatment, the best food he had ever had in a hospital, but he couldn't eat. The trauma left him with no appetite. He was in good spirits, as he always is, but something in his system changed for that time period. A part of him was gone and could not be replaced with a new leg. But the Lord was good;, and friends and family were there for us.

On Friday, October 27, Jerry was transferred to Joan Glancy Rehabilitation Center, where I got my first view of the wound that was left from the amputation. He went through exercises to learn how to get into and out of a shower, how to manage a wheel chair, and a walker, and how to get into and out of a car. He is blessed to have no steps between our garage and the back door. Who would have known when I designed the house, and it was built eleven years before, with wide doors and hallway, that this would be the reason. The Lord is so good to know these things before we do, and to provide for us.

Home Health Care

We came home from rehab on Wednesday, November 8, with a wheel chair, a walker, and a bench for the tub ~ not much of an exchange for a leg, but blessings. Our next hope was for healing, so that he could be fitted for the prosthesis.

We were set up for physical therapy and wound care at home. Jerry soon took the responsibility for his physical therapy. (I have noticed that I have used the pronoun we, instead of he. In these times, it is as if it was all happening to me. Jerry doesn't remember any of the details.)

The first night Jerry was home I brought dinner to him in bed; I actually thanked him for letting me serve him. I cannot explain the joy of serving, as unto the Lord. There will be times when it will be more of a hardship than others, but my prayer is to continue always in a *meek and quiet spirit*, wherein is the joy.

Every day, for two and a half months, a visiting health nurse came to change the dressings. The incision at the knee from the first surgery produced a tunnel that had to be packed. A new wound formed where the flap met the amputation below the knee, which had to be packed, and after a few weeks with the removable plastic cast a pressure ulcer formed. All three wounds were "yucky," as our 3½-year-old granddaughter Emma called it. She would come to the hospital with Lee, our daughter, and with me on the days I was caring for her, when we went to sit with Jerry. She was experiencing all of this with us as I continued to care for her.

Knowing that one day I would have to take care of this large wound, I watched studiously as the nurse unwrapped the stump, disposed of the materials, cleaned the wound, packed it, and dressed it again. I was not used to such a sight, nor was I looking forward to this duty as a caregiver. One day the nurse came, and said, "It's your turn." Totally unexpected, I didn't know what to say, or to do. But the Lord blessed to guide me, even though I was oblivious to what I was doing. The nurse's duty was over, and mine had just begun. We were still going every two weeks to the wound treatment center, and when we thought the wound was healed we made an appointment for a fitting for a "new leg."

We went for physical therapy and instructions for using the prosthesis, and Jerry tried wearing it, only to open up the wound again.

For 3 ½ years I cleaned and redressed the part of the wound that would not heal. We were back at the wound treatment center numerous times. In many visits to the surgeon we could get only one answer, "It will take time." Blood and bandages were all that we knew every day until Andy talked to a doctor that practiced at Emory, who suggested that we see the new surgeon. Andy made the appointment for us with another surgeon. We acquired Jerry's records from the previous surgeon. Quickly looking through these records the night before our appointment, we read the last remark from our last office visit, "Avoid surgery, at all costs." The first surgeon had said he never wanted to put a knife to Jerry's leg for any reason. He was afraid that another wound would not heal.

(During this period there seemed to be a correlation between the division in our church and Jerry's amputation. The healing for both was something that we prayed and waited for. Both came almost simultaneously.)

New Surgeon, New Hope

Our first visit with the new surgeon gave us hope. In his sixties, he was a confident doctor who had seen almost everything to do with this type of surgery. He asked if Jerry had a graft. We said, "What is a graft?" His assistant, who had been reviewing the records, handed them to the surgeon, where he had opened them to a certain page. He said, "You have a graft." We were unaware that this graft was part of the by-pass surgery that the first surgeon did.

He had never had a patient whose body had rejected a graft, but said that 2% of patients cannot tolerate them. He suggested that this was Jerry's problem, and wanted to do another surgery. So, on September 13, 2010, in a four-hour surgery, the graft was removed, leaving a fifteen-inch scar from Jerry's groan to his knee. The surgeon could not guarantee that this would be the answer to healing, but we all had hope.

After the surgery I was taking care of two wounds. As with the first surgery, the end of the new incision was not healing. Instead of our scheduled March appointment, we had an appointment in January, at which time the surgeon had no answer for us. He said that he did not think that either the old wound, or the new wound was going to heal. The only way he could help from that point was to do an amputation above the knee. He also told us that he did not have an elderly patient that was able to use a prosthesis.

Having been told about bariatric healing, and doing some research, I asked him if he knew anything about it. He said that there had not been any proof that it works. We left his office discouraged and helpless. After another week or so of changing dressings on both wounds, and the new wound becoming larger and larger, I made an appointment with Jerry's primary physician. He agreed to send us to the Bariatric Center in Gainesville, a thirty-minute drive, to see what they would suggest.

Wound Treatment

This being a wound treatment center, the doctor and nurses first evaluated the wounds; then did a test to see if Jerry was a candidate for bariatric treatment. He was not eligible, because the test showed that he had circulation to the area of the wounds. Bariatric treatment provides oxygen to the part of the body that needs healing. We learned that it was not oxygen that he needed, but proper wound care. From the first visit we were assured that both wounds could be healed. The wound specialist, who was also a surgeon, thought that the surgeon was right in his diagnosis and procedure to remove the graft. Where he thought he failed was in not offering wound treatment. The irony, we discovered, was that the nurses who were experienced in the practice of wound care received their training at Emory.

Beginning in February, Jerry received wound treatment for both wounds; one healed faster than the other, and on July 7 we were discharged. Once a week we had driven to the center; two other days a visiting nurse came to our home for treatment. Driving home after our last appointment we praised the Lord for his intervention in the healing; first in directing us to the wound treatment center. The staff had become like family to us. During those months I talked with the wife of an 85-year-old patient who was receiving bariatric treatment for his amputation wound that had not healed. He was still a patient there when Jerry was discharged, but months later she told me in a phone conversation that her husband's leg had healed and that he was wearing his prosthesis all day with no problems.

The New Leg

We were advised to wait a few weeks before making an appointment for a fitting for a new prosthesis. Before healing Jerry could never wear a shrinker-hose. Now that the wounds had healed he wore the hose and the stump shrunk, so he needed a new liner and prosthesis. Again we had appointments for physical therapy and training to learn to walk with the prosthesis. The Lord blessed that we did not have to go to Gainesville, but to a facility closer to home.

Jerry received the normal quota for therapy and was able to finally walk using a walker. Because of the soreness that he still experiences, he is only able to "wear the leg" when he goes out. I encouraged him to do the driving again. At first he was hesitant, after so long a time. He is comfortable again driving locally. Even though he was driving to Thomaston and back to see our families, he now is a little leery of this. He does well in a wheelchair at home; and is able to care for most of his own personal needs. He used to help with the cooking, and I did the cleaning, but now both are my responsibility. He does, however, help with chopping, mixing, etc. The low bar in the kitchen is convenient for this. Serving both our plates has become a normal activity at mealtime. It is not unusual for me to eat while I am standing or doing something else in the kitchen. Eating food that is cold is not a problem anymore, although I am better able now to plan so that I can eat at the same time with Jerry.

Weeds, Poop, and Laughter

Since Jerry's last surgery, wound treatment and healing, the Lord has blessed us with good times together. He has never been a worrier, and never complains, always taking things as they come; which has made it so much easier for me. The Lord blessed Jerry with a quick wit; thankfully, he did not lose his sense of humor when he lost his leg. He keeps me laughing. He is always grateful, thanking me for everything I do. I have learned, from Chick-fil-A, to say, "You are welcome; it's my pleasure." We have laughed more, and worried less, even through other difficult situations.

I recall thinking that we ought to downsize again, and move to a smaller house with less yard maintenance. We have had someone to keep the lawn cut since Jerry's first surgery. Other things, like pruning shrubbery, I have been doing myself.

I was very discouraged one day when I was on my knees tackling the weeds. Stopping before I was barely started I walked in the house and told Jerry that I didn't think it was God's will for me to spend the rest of my life pulling weeds. God proved His will over mine when Jerry decided to refinance the house.

Since then weeds and I still don't get along well together, but the Lord has shown me how to take them as they come, and to praise Him for them.

They are still part of my training. In different ways I have learned a lot from gardening and laughed much in the process. One day I came in from working outside to the screened back porch, where Jerry spends a lot of his time. I told him, "There is poop on the back grass." Sitting innocently in his wheelchair he immediately and calmly stated, "I didn't do it."

The Ultimate Caregiver

I wish I could express what the Lord has been doing, and is still doing, in my heart and life. To give my life for others would never have been my choice. It was His choice, first by giving His life for me, being the example, opening my heart and eyes to true life in love and service to Him.

I grew up with a selfish, rebellious spirit. Even as a child, baptized into the church at the age of eleven, my will was not relinquished to the Lord's will. My life did not change until He changed my heart. In the story of my life (the longer version) *Red Clover and Silver Tap Shoes* I go into depth as to His working from age to age; and from curtains to stages, as He has revealed Himself to me ~ how He bought me, sought me, caught me, brought me, and taught me.

The greatest thing on earth is to love the Lord with all my heart, all my soul, all my mind, and all my strength, and my neighbor as myself. This comes only by knowing His love for me, expressed in 1 John 4:10, *Herein is love; not that we loved God, but that He first loved us, and gave His Son to be a propitiation for us.*

What is our response to His love? John tells us this, also. *Hereby perceive we the love of God, because he laid down his life for us: and we ought to lay down our lives for the brethren.* 1 John 3:16

I could not perceive laying down my life for someone else until I was brought to understand the truth of the depth of God's love in laying down His life for me. It still astounds me today to think of this "great salvation" that is ours in Christ. (Hebrews 2) He set the example, opened the path, calls us to follow His example, and leads us in the way of humility and sacrifice. For me there is no true life apart from Him and His leading. He is the true Shepherd, who cares for His sheep. We have experienced His care during times of adversity, when we in our weakness and distress, have been recipients of His mercy and grace.

In dealing with Jerry's handicap I learned of my own handicaps, and came to lean on and trust the Lord more and more. It is true, even today, when Jerry does not need me as much as he did after his amputation. My physical needs are greater than before; I have experienced what the apostle Paul expressed in his second letter to the Corinthian church ~ *though the outward man perish, yet the inward man is renewed day by day.* The following references from God's Word were used for my dad's funeral; I have not been able to forget them.

For all things are for your sakes, that the abundant grace might through the thanksgiving of many redound to the glory of God. For which cause we faint not; but though our outward man perish, yet the inward man is renewed day by day. For our light affliction, which is but for a moment, worketh for us a far more exceeding and eternal weight of glory; While we look not at the things which are seen, but at the things which are not seen: for the things which are seen are temporal; but the things which are not seen are eternal. 2 Corinthians 4: 15-18

My service to Mother, Jerry, my family, and my church are for the same purpose as Paul's ~ for God's glory, our thanksgiving and joy. The Lord has blessed for me to continue to serve in different ways in our church. Still needed as pianist until a year ago I had time to practice during the week; to be *a keeper at home*, with minimal work in the yard. At this particular time, I am experiencing the Lord's work in disciplining me, and ordering my time for writing. I must still be aware of my first priority as Jerry's wife/caregiver ~ as unto the Lord. All else is beside this point.   It is always easy to be distracted, detained, and deceived into spending time in my own exploits.

The Four Corners of My World

Years ago the realization of boundaries set me to thinking of where the Lord was leading me to spend my time; time that I saw as borrowed, time that was His, and not mine. This came in a diagram that I labeled The Four Corners of My World ~ Husband, Home, Family, and Church. This was the order based on which was closest to me. Home came second because I have this responsibility every day. Family came third because I don't see them, nor talk to them every day. Church came fourth because I am not as involved as I used to be. In the center of all is Christ ~ His cross, the sacrifice, grace and righteousness that works out in all areas of my life. Christ as the center, my Shepherd, my all, enables me to do the will of the Father, working His Holy Spirit within me. He gives an awareness of the needs of others. As Jerry's caregiver I can sometimes anticipate his needs before he does.

Chapter 7

STILL LEARNING

For I have learned,
in whatsoever state I am,
therewith to be content.
Philippians 4:11

Until the Lord shows us something different we are settled into our routines. Jerry and I are doing all that we can, physically, and praying daily for wisdom, grace, and strength, for all that He wants us to do to witness of His grace, His presence and His power. We started using jigsaw puzzles with Mother when she was living with us. Jerry and I have graduated from 100 to 1000 piece puzzles; we always keep one going on the dining room table.

The children and grandchildren fill in some of the pieces when they are here. Each day can present a new challenge but we are still learning that the Lord is good, *Oh, that men would praise Him for His goodness, and His wonderful works to the children of men.* Psalm 107:8

As I *grow in grace and the knowledge of our Lord Jesus Christ,* I am continuing to study and desire the humility of Christ and contentment in Him. Andrew Murray's book on *Humility* is a good source that has helped me with this, which in 2014 I shared in monthly posts on my blog. Thomas Watson's book, *The Art of Divine Contentment,* is a wonderful book that I continue to study; and pray for the Lord's work in me.

His

I believe that God created me to be Jerry's helpmate. It has taken all these years for me to see and understand this. There is a popular book, written for wives, titled *Created to be His Helpmate.* When I saw it I thought that a simpler expression, "created to be his" summed up the whole matter of my life. My life is meant to be a counterpart of Jerry's life. As I continue to *follow Christ, in denying myself, and taking up my cross daily,* He is also showing me that I was created to be His. This has all worked out in my care for Jerry; *as unto the Lord.* Giving up my own life has not been easy, but God's plan for my creation and redemption was for this purpose. I desire with all my heart to have a heart for sacrifice and service only for Him. Being a caregiver is not a natural desire, but a calling from the Lord; a holy, heavenly, high calling that only He can prepare us for, to lead us in his own footsteps, and to guide us with His own hand. The Psalmist in Psalm 138:8 prays that the Lord *forsake not the works of Thine own hands* ~ understanding that all service in His name is His own work in and through the servant. The prayer in Psalm 90:17 *Let the beauty of the Lord be upon us, and establish thou the work of our hands upon us.* is recognition that He works through us. The work of His *own hands* is His power at work in *our hands* for His kingdom.

Isolated but Content

Caregivers and the ones for whom we care are often isolated. We are not involved in activities that we once enjoyed. Because of Jerry's amputation, and able only to wear his prosthesis for short periods of time, we are not able to travel as we used to. He cannot climb more than one step and cannot sit for long periods of time. This keeps us home most of the time, but we have learned to be content where God has placed us. He is more than able to supply all our needs, and more than we need, since we are completely dependent on Him. Our joy is in Him, not in what we could be doing, or where we could be going.

Having more time at home gives me the opportunity to read and to write of His goodness and His grace. My thoughts and praises are sometimes shared on my blog, God's Grace ~ God's Glory. I have more opportunity for prayer. *In Prayer and In Touch* is a ministry of intercession that I do through emails.

Cleaning My Plates

I have discussed with Jerry some of what I have been writing in this little book. When we talked about how you eat all that is on your plate ~ what we or someone else has put on it ~ we agreed that it is by taking "one bite at the time." All is for a purpose, and not to be wasted, everything working *together for our good*; that we may be *conformed to the image of Christ*. (Romans 8:28-29) With this concept I am learning to take not only "one day at a time" but each moment as it comes, using each day more perceptively, planning a little here, a little there. "One a day" is a medical term for taking pills, but I am using it to accomplish what needs to be done. I explain this in detail in another Little Book, *Focus, Balance, and Order ~ Three Facets of the Christian Life*.

Continuing to Follow the Master Caregiver

A daily walk with Christ is required to continue in service where He wills us to be. The following are Scripture references that remind me of who I am as His servant. I must sit at Jesus' feet and learn from Him if I am to serve Him. I must pray, not only for Jerry and me, but also for all saints and Christ's church. I must participate in weekly worship, serving Him and His people.

If I am to fulfill His will for my creation and redemption ∼ Christ's dying for me ∼ everything must be for His glory; the chief end ∼ *to glorify Him and enjoy Him forever.* (Shorter Catechism)The joy comes as He is being glorified in me.

*If I then, your Lord and Master, have washed your feet;
ye also ought to wash one another's feet.*
John 13:14

Christ has not only washed my feet, but sanctifies me *by the washing of the water by the word.* (Ephesians 5:26) We minister to others because He has ministered to us, personally. We serve others because He has served us. We seek always to learn of Him and follow in His footsteps.

Thomas Watson in his book, *The Art of Divine Contentment*, says, "To learn Christ is to live Christ. When we have Bible conduct, our lives, like rich diamonds, cast a sparkling luster in the church of God (Philippians 1:27), and are, in some sense, parallel with the life of Christ, as the transcript is to the original." But this is all His work, not ours, for without Him we can do nothing.

And whosoever will be chief among you, let him be your servant: Even as the Son of man came not to be ministered unto, but to minister, and to give his life a ransom for many. Matthew 20:28

The disciple is not above his master, nor the servant above his lord. Matthew 10:24

We are healed and cleansed that we may minister.

And he came and took her by the hand, and lifted her up; and she ministered unto them. Mark 1:31

All is God's will, His calling, and His gift; for His glory and praise.

If any man speak, let him speak as the oracles of God; if any man minister, let him do it as of the ability which God giveth: that God in all things may be glorified through Jesus Christ, to whom be praise and dominion for ever and ever. Amen. 1 Peter 4:11

The work here, and the end of all things, is that we may serve Him forever. I believe that the purpose of this life, His calling and gifts, are to prepare us for an eternal glory with Him.

And there shall be no more curse:
but the throne of God and of the Lamb shall be in it;
and his servants shall serve him.
Revelation 22:3

In this world or the next there is no greater life than to be His servant. What a glorious day, when worship and service to Him will be the height of our glory in His kingdom. We have yet to learn all that He is waiting to teach us.

Chapter 8

ENCOURAGEMENT FOR CAREGIVERS

Blessed be God,
Who comforteth us in all our tribulation,
that we may be able to comfort them
which are in any trouble, by the comfort wherewith we
ourselves are comforted of God.
2 Corinthians 1:3-4

No one is ready for the role of caregiver, no matter how well we have served in other areas. When the time comes we do it, because it is our calling at a particular time in our lives. This role usually falls on members of the immediate family ~ husband for wife, or wife for husband; sometimes, children for a parent, and parent for a child.

The first thing needed is love. It is hoped that when the time comes for you to fill this role, you already love the person for whom you must care. The love of the caregiver is stronger than the need. Sometimes this love must overcome the obstacles. When the person to be cared for is not cooperative, and even somewhat abusive, the caregiver's love can overcome the temptation to react, and so, in wisdom know how to work through the difficult situation.

As caregivers we must pray with faith, believing that the love of our heavenly Father, and our Lord Jesus Christ will work in us, by the power of the Holy Spirit, doing what we cannot do in our own heart and strength. We will find that we are receiving what we need for ourselves and for those for whom we care.

Take heart by knowing that you are not the only person who has had to care for a loved one during the most difficult time in their lives. For the spouse it is the fulfilling of a marriage vow that we took when we began our life journey together. "For better or worse" doesn't seem to take on its true meaning until we come to this stage in our marriage. We, who are the "older" generation, understand this better than recent generations, where most marriages don't make it to this stage.

Major Decisions

There are times when the spouse or child is not capable, or able, to care for their loved one. This is the case when the spouse needs to aid in his or her mobility. When the spouse is not in good health, outside help is needed. To keep the patient in the home may be the best for them, but may not be the best for the caregiver.   Prayer and counseling are needed in making these decisions.

If the patient is physically abusive there needs to be counseling to make the decision for the best care. If it is a matter of dealing with the emotional aspect of the situation, everything needs to be weighed and prayed through.   To care for a loved one, even under emotional upheaval, makes us stronger.   Sometimes God does give us more than we can bear, so that we draw near to Him, to know His care for us, to prove us, and grow us in these difficult times.

The Challenge

Everything new that seems to be impossible can be either of two things: a *challenge* we will not accept, nor deal with; or an *opportunity* to see how God works through us.   If we will not accept the challenge, nothing else needs to be said. If we accept the role of caregiver, we have an opportunity of helping make the last days of someone else's life better than it would be without us.

The challenge of being a caregiver far outweighs other opportunities in this life and lays up treasures for us in heaven. When we think of how much the Lord gave up for us, what more can we do than give all that we have for those we love. The life of a caregiver is a definite calling. We not only find ourselves in the place of service, but the Lord also gives the provisions that are needed. He does not call us, expecting that we can handle this role on our own, but it is a time to experience His presence, His wisdom, and His strength. As our needs draw us closer to Him, we not only see that we "do what we have to do," but that we do more than we thought we could do.

There is a supernatural working in the life of a Christian caregiver. Christ enables us to minister to others unselfishly, as His Spirit is in us, working through us.

Paul speaks of wives submitting to their husbands, *as unto the Lord.* (Ephesians 5:22) Would this not also relate to caring for our husbands in their time of need?

The person for whom we care is the person Jesus speaks of in Matthew 25:40. *Inasmuch as ye have done it unto one of the least of these my brethren, ye have done it unto me.* In both the caregiver, and the one being cared for, the Lord is represented. He is both the giver and the receiver. All is by His working and all for Him and His glory. Research will avail us ways that we can spend time with our loved one, time that we might not have spent with them if all was well. Jerry and I would never have chosen to spend time putting jigsaw puzzles together, but it has become a joy for me to have this time with him.

We Are Not Alone

As caregivers we are not alone. As we take each day that comes, as well prepared as we can be in our walk with the Lord, in prayer and with His promises in hand and heart, we are sometimes blessed beyond measure. Sometimes we may fail to rise to the challenge as we should, or as we would want to, but the Lord has promised to always be with us. It is these times of our lives when God is the most real to us. It is when we need Him the most that we know His presence and His power.

There are others who are ready and available to help, in the medical field, in our church, and our family. There are books, there are support groups; there is more than we know, because we have not needed these before. After you have been through this experience God will use you to minister to someone else.

My prayer is that your heart will take courage from the Lord, that you will know the Lord's will for your life in the matter of caring for your loved one, that He will give you grace, wisdom and strength as you face the days or years ahead. Remember, that this is only temporary. What legacy will you leave with this episode of your life?

The Lord bless you and keep you,
and cause His face to shine upon you
and be gracious to you; and give you peace.
Numbers 6:26

Chapter 9

OTHER CAREGIVERS

Linda became a friend through a relationship at our church. Getting to know her and the "potholes" she has been through has been a blessing for me. Through her testimony I know that I am not the only one who has come to love and trust the Savior and to experience His gracious presence during the difficult times. She too was given the wisdom and strength to care for her loved ones when they could not care for themselves.

"Life is a road. The decisions we make at a crossroad and how we handle potholes make a big difference. Over time, and making many wrong decisions, I realized that without the Lord I could not survive. With His forgiveness and my repentance I now walk with the Father and He guides my life. Through much prayer He has given me strength. This was experienced when our eight-year-old son was diagnosed with Duchene Muscular Dystrophy.

Did I accept that my child had been given a death sentence? At first I would sit and watch him breathe. I expected him to die at any moment. Then, instead of wasting the time, I realized how fortunate we were in this opportunity to make the best of the time we had with him.

Through continued prayer the Lord confirmed His presence with us through it all. I wanted to pray for a complete recovery, but accepted that it was not probable; it was a genetic defect he was born with.

So, I prayed and God gave me strength and understanding for myself, and a productive life for my son; I saw this as His work in our lives for His purpose. He gave us this precious time as a gift for us to enjoy Eric.

In those fifteen years we traveled and were involved in raising money for research. We were honored with a trip via Make-A-Wish, acted as a sponsor for MDA, and Eric was able to attend MDA Camp each year. His fifteenth birthday would have been his first day in heaven --- he died the day before his birthday. Even more than knowing his likes, his dislikes, his dreams, personality and his

BIG brown eyes, we knew that he had been baptized and that he knew the Lord Jesus.

It has been many years since we lost Eric; and the acceptance of God's will was NOT immediate. Even though I knew it would happen, I was not prepared for another heartache. I went through many months of sorrow and anger. I was mad at God, and for a time I simply stopped praying.

It was not until I started praying again that I was able to accept Eric's death as God's will. He was with me through those times and forgave me for doubting Him."

(Linda has also been a caregiver for her husband and her mother. A few weeks before her husband died she was diagnosed with lung cancer. She is undergoing chemotherapy, lives alone, and praises the Lord for each new day. She is now the recipient of care from others as she waits with hope and joy for the new heavens and new earth.)

There are others that I know personally who have been caregivers for spouses, and some who have been caring for their handicapped children for many years who also give God the glory for His grace and strength.

Fran Rogers   August 28, 2013 (New Birth date)

Update at time of drafting this book for publication:

Linda died on September 21. 2015. I wept with her family, but I rejoiced with her as she was prepared to enter the Master's presence.

On December 28, 2015 Jerry went into cardiac arrest as he was being transported to the hospital with congestive heart failure due to a kidney infection. Again the Lord blessed to be with us during this time. While spending a week in the hospital, we had the opportunity to talk to others about the goodness of the Lord.

We are still learning that the role of a caregiver is bound up in the word "give." The Lord gives abundantly from the "riches of His glory" for all our needs. From Him we know the source of all care and are enabled to care for others.

The older we are, the more we praise Him. The more adversity we experience, the more we sense God's presence and power.

The more we give, the more He replenishes. And His love goes on and on and on ~ ~ ~ ~

Acknowledgements:

The Lord has blessed to give me family and friends for encouragement while preparing our books for publishing. SPECIAL THANKS go to my daughter Lee for her support, and her proofing, and to Margaret Beville for editing TWO FULL PLATES.

Books especially for the caregiver of those with failing memory:

Forgetting Whose We Are   Alzheimer's Disease and the Love of God   David Keck
At the Heart of Alzheimer's   Carol Simpson
Loving Care for Alzheimer's Patients   Practical Solutions for Caregivers and their Families Katie Lovette
The 36-Hour Day   A Family Guide to Caring for Person's with Alzheimer Disease, Related Dementing Illnesses, and Memory Loss in Later Life   Nancy L. Mac

About the Author

Fran Rogers is a wife/caregiver to Jerry, her husband of 55 years, a 77-year-old mother of two, grandmother of six, and a great-grandmother, writer and blogger in Buford, Georgia. She writes from the experience of enduring many difficulties while living in the reality of God's grace. By His Spirit and through God's Word she has learned to be dependent on Him for all things, witnessing His love, joy, and goodness. Writing for over twenty-five years, she is now beginning to publish what God has been teaching her. The purpose of her writing is to share with God's people the legacy of His kingdom. She is a witness of God's provisions for all things of this life, and even more; the eternal life that He has prepared for all His people. The majority of proceeds from sales will be given to charity and to missions that witness of God's kingdom throughout this world. In view of Christ's promise that He would have witnesses in *Jerusalem, Judea, and Samaria, and to the uttermost part of the earth,* her hope is that God's people who read will not only benefit, but also promote this message to others through their purchase. See the website fatherandfamily.com for more details of this ministry.

Other books are available, published, or soon to be published, in the series *Little Books About the Magnitude of God*; her work is longer than an article, but not as extensive as a regular length book. Most could be read in one sitting, except for Bible studies or devotionals.

Website: fatherandfamily.com
Blog: godsgracegodsglory.com
Facebook: Father and Family Books
Contact: contact@fatherandfamily.com

Little Books About the Magnitude of God
*(Published *)*

FIRST THINGS That Last FOREVER
*The Garden of GOD'S WORD~ The Purpose and
Delight of BIBLE STUDY*
*The LITTLE BOAT and other
Short Stories of GOD'S GRACE*
Child Keeping ~ God's Blessing to Parents
Prayers That Brought the House Down
One Month to Live ~ A Father's Last Words
A Broad Review of Andrew Murray's "Humility"
Notes on Paul's Letter to the Romans
Legacy of the Seven Psalms + One
God's Grace ~ God's Glory

What the Holy Bible Says
What the Holy BIBLE Says About LIGHT
What the Holy Bible Says About GOD'S WORD
What the Holy Bible Says About LIFE

Other Books
Waiting is Not a Game~ Articles of Faith
My Garden and other Poems of GOD'S GRACE

www.ingramcontent.com/pod-product-compliance
Lightning Source LLC
Chambersburg PA
CBHW020513030426
42337CB00011B/373